The Usborne
First book of
Christmas
Carols

Models made by Jo Litchfield

Designed by Helen Wood

Photography by Howard Allman
Carol arrangements by Eileen O'Brien

With thanks to Staedtler for providing the Fimo® material for models.

Away in a Manger

The cattle are lowing, the baby awakes,
But little Lord Jesus, no crying he makes.
I love thee Lord Jesus; look down from the sky,
And stay by my side until morning is nigh.

Ding dong! Merrily on High

Ding dong! Mer-ri-ly on high, In heav'n the bells are ring-ing,

Ding dong! Ve-ri-ly the sky Is riv'n with an-gels sing-ing.

Glo - - - - - - - ri-a, Ho-

-san - na in ex - cel - sis. cel - sis.

And on earth below, below,
Let steeple bells be swungen,
And i-o, i-o, i-o,
By priest and people sungen.

Gloria, Hosanna in excelsis.
Gloria, Hosanna in excelsis.

Pray you, dutifully prime
Your matin chime, you ringers,
May you beautifully rhyme
Your eve-time song, you singers.

Gloria, Hosanna in excelsis.
Gloria, Hosanna in excelsis.

Deck the Hall with Boughs of Holly

Deck   the hall with boughs of hol - ly,   Fa la la la la,   la

la la la, 'Tis the sea - son   to be jol - ly,   Fa la la la la,   la

la la la,   Don   we now our   gay   ap - pa - rel,

Fa la la,   la la la,   la   la   la,   Troll   the an - cient

Yule - tide car - ol,   Fa la la la la,   la la la la.

See the blazing Yule before us,
Fa la la la la, la la la la,
Strike the harp and join the chorus,
Fa la la la la, la la la la,
Follow me in merry measure,
Fa la la, la la la, la la la,
While I tell of Yuletide treasure,
Fa la la la la, la la la la.

Fast away the old year passes,
Fa la la la la, la la la la,
Hail the new, ye lads and lasses,
Fa la la la la, la la la la,
Sing we joyous all together,
Fa la la, la la la, la la la,
Heedless of the wind and weather,
Fa la la la la, la la la la.

While Shepherds Watched Their Flocks

While shep-herds watched their flocks by night, All seat-ed on the ground, The an-gel of the Lord came down, And glor-y shone a-round.

"Fear not," said he; for mighty dread
Had seized their troubled mind;
"Glad tidings of great joy I bring
To you and all mankind.

"To you in David's town this day
Is born of David's line
A Saviour, who is Christ the Lord;
And this shall be the sign:

"The heavenly Babe you there shall find
To human view displayed
All meanly wrapped in swathing bands,
And in a manger laid."

We Three Kings of Orient Are

Glorious now behold him arise,
King and God and sacrifice,
Alleluia, Alleluia;
Earth to the heavens replies.

O star of wonder, star of night,
Star with royal beauty bright,
Westward leading, still proceeding,
Guide us to thy perfect light.

The Holly and the Ivy

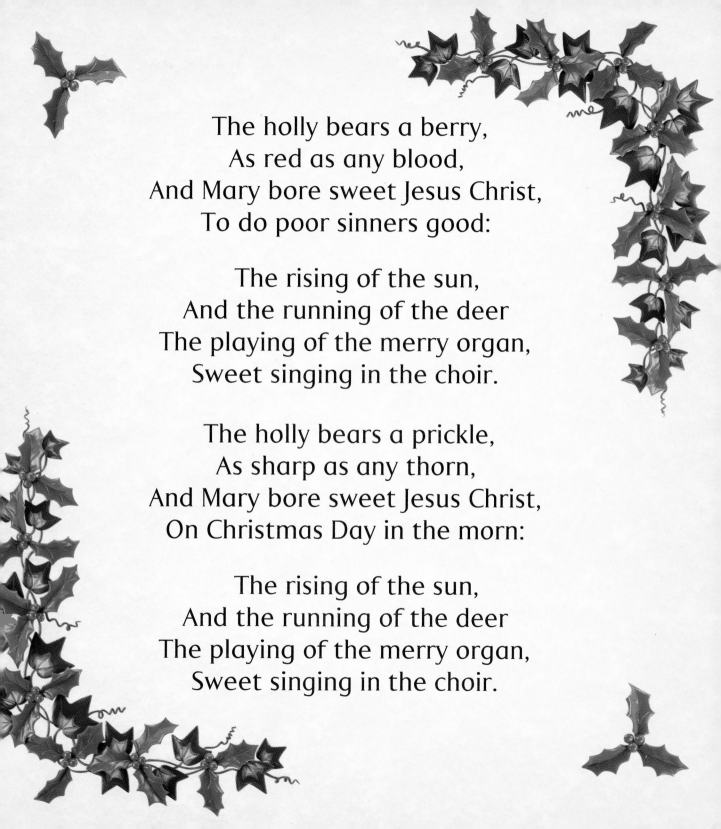

The holly bears a berry,
As red as any blood,
And Mary bore sweet Jesus Christ,
To do poor sinners good:

The rising of the sun,
And the running of the deer
The playing of the merry organ,
Sweet singing in the choir.

The holly bears a prickle,
As sharp as any thorn,
And Mary bore sweet Jesus Christ,
On Christmas Day in the morn:

The rising of the sun,
And the running of the deer
The playing of the merry organ,
Sweet singing in the choir.

Hark! The Herald Angels Sing

Christ, by highest heaven adored,
Christ, the everlasting Lord,
Late in time behold him come,
Offspring of a Virgin's womb.
Veiled in flesh the Godhead see;
Hail, the Incarnate Deity,
Pleased as Man with man to dwell,
Jesus, our Emmanuel!

Hark! the herald angels sing,
"Glory to the new-born King."

Silent Night

Silent night, holy night,
Shepherds wake at the sight;
Glory streams from heaven afar,
Heavenly hosts sing Alleluia.
Christ the Saviour is born!
Christ the Saviour is born!

O Come, All Ye Faithful

God of God,
Light of Light,
Lo! He abhors not the Virgin's womb;
Very God,
Begotten, not created:

O come let us adore him...

Sing, choirs of angels,
Sing in exultation,
Sing, all you citizens of heaven above;
Glory to God
In the highest:

O come let us adore him...

O Little Town of Bethlehem

O lit -tle town of Beth - le - hem, How still we__ see thee

lie. A - bove thy deep and dream - less__ sleep, The

si - lent__ stars go by. Yet__ in thy dark__ streets__

shi — neth The ev - er -last-ing light. The hopes and fears of

all__ the__ years Are met in__ thee to - night.

O morning stars, together
Proclaim thy holy birth.
And praises sing to God the King
And peace to men on earth.
For Christ is born of Mary
And, gathered all above,
While mortals sleep, the angels keep
Their watch of wondering love.

We Wish You a Merry Christmas

We all want some figgy pudding,
We all want some figgy pudding,
We all want some figgy pudding,
So bring some right here!

Good tidings we bring
To you and your kin;
We wish you a merry Christmas
And a happy New Year.

We won't go until we get some,
We won't go until we get some,
We won't go until we get some,
So bring some right here!

Good tidings we bring
To you and your kin;
We wish you a merry Christmas
And a happy New Year.

First published in 2003 by Usborne Publishing Ltd, 83-85 Saffron Hill, London ECIN 8RT, England. www.usborne.com
Copyright © 2003 Usborne Publishing Ltd. The name Usborne and the devices ♛ ⊕ are Trade Marks of Usborne Publishing Ltd.